I0448511

September 2013

CIVIL SUPPORT

Actions Are Needed to Improve DOD's Planning for a Complex Catastrophe

September 2013

GAO Highlights

Highlights of GAO-13-763, a report to Congressional Requesters

CIVIL SUPPORT

Actions Are Needed to Improve DOD's Planning for a Complex Catastrophe

Why GAO Did This Study

The United States continues to face an uncertain and complicated security environment, as major disasters and emergencies, such as the Boston Marathon bombings and Hurricane Sandy illustrate. DOD supports civil authorities' response to domestic incidents through an array of activities collectively termed civil support. In July 2012, DOD began to plan for federal military support during a complex catastrophe—such as a large earthquake that causes extraordinary levels of casualties or damage, and cascading failures of critical infrastructure. GAO was asked to assess DOD's planning and capabilities for a complex catastrophe. This report assesses the extent to which DOD has (1) planned for and identified capabilities to respond to complex catastrophes, and (2) established a command and control construct for complex catastrophes and other multistate incidents. To do so, GAO analyzed civil support plans, guidance, and other documents, and interviewed DOD and FEMA officials.

What GAO Recommends

GAO recommends that combatant commands (1) work through the defense coordinating officers to develop an interim set of specific DOD capabilities that could be provided to prepare for and respond to complex catastrophes, as FEMA completes its five-year regional planning cycle; and (2) develop, clearly define, communicate, and implement a construct for the command and control of federal military forces during multistate civil support incidents such as complex catastrophes. DOD concurred with both recommendations.

View GAO-13-763. For more information, contact Brian Lepore at (202) 512-4523 or leporeb@gao.gov.

What GAO Found

U.S. Northern Command (NORTHCOM) and U.S. Pacific Command (PACOM) are updating their existing civil support plans to include a complex catastrophe scenario, as directed by the Secretary of Defense and the Joint Staff. However, the commands are delaying the identification of capabilities that could be provided to execute the plans until the Federal Emergency Management Agency (FEMA), the lead federal response agency, completes its regional planning efforts in 2018. NORTHCOM officials told us that the command's civil support plan would describe some general force requirements, such as types of military units, but that it will not identify specific capabilities that could be provided to civil authorities during a complex catastrophe. Similarly, according to PACOM officials, PACOM's plan also will not identify such capabilities. Still, defense coordinating officers—senior military officers who work closely with federal, state, and local officials in FEMA's regional offices—have taken some initial steps to coordinate with FEMA during its regional planning process to identify capabilities that the Department of Defense (DOD) may be required to provide in some regions. For example, a defense coordinating officer has helped one of the FEMA regions that has completed its regional plan to develop bundled mission assignments that pre-identify a group of capabilities that region will require during a complex catastrophe. DOD doctrine states that the department should interact with non-DOD agencies to gain a mutual understanding of their response capabilities and limitations. By working through the defense coordinating officers to identify an interim set of specific capabilities for a complex catastrophe—instead of waiting for FEMA to complete its five-year regional planning process—NORTHCOM and PACOM can enhance their preparedness and mitigate the risk of an unexpected capability gap during the five-year period until FEMA completes its regional plans in 2018.

DOD has established a command and control framework for a federal military civil support response; however, the command and control structure for federal military forces during complex catastrophes is unclear because DOD has not developed a construct prescribing the roles, responsibilities, and relationships among command elements that may be involved in responding to such incidents across multiple states. This gap in the civil support framework was illustrated by recent events such as National Level Exercise 2011—which examined DOD's response to a complex catastrophe—and the federal military response to Hurricane Sandy in 2012. For example, officials from NORTHCOM's Army component told us that the exercise revealed that the absence of an operational-level command element created challenges for NORTHCOM in managing the operations of federal military forces during a large-scale, multistate incident. Similarly, DOD after action reports on Hurricane Sandy found that the command and control structure for federal military forces was not clearly defined, resulting in the degradation of situational awareness and unity of effort, and the execution of missions without proper approval. DOD doctrine states that operational plans should identify the command structure expected to exist during their implementation. By identifying roles, responsibilities, and command relationships during multistate incidents such as complex catastrophes, DOD will be better positioned to manage and allocate resources across a multistate area and ensure effective and organized response operations.

_____ United States Government Accountability Office

Contents

Abbreviations

DOD	Department of Defense
FEMA	Federal Emergency Management Agency
NORTHCOM	U.S. Northern Command
PACOM	U.S. Pacific Command

GAO U.S. GOVERNMENT ACCOUNTABILITY

441 G St. N.W.
Washington, DC 20548

September 30, 2013

The Honorable Thomas R. Carper
Chairman
The Honorable Tom Coburn, M.D.
Ranking Member
Committee on Homeland Security and Governmental Affairs
United States Senate

The Honorable Susan M. Collins
United States Senate

The United States continues to face an uncertain and complicated security environment with the potential for major disasters and emergencies,[1] as incidents such as the Boston Marathon bombings, Hurricane Sandy, and recent wildfires illustrate. DOD supports civil authorities' response to domestic incidents through an array of activities collectively termed civil support.[2] After the September 11, 2001 terrorist attacks, the Department of Defense (DOD) established U.S. Northern Command (NORTHCOM) in October 2002 to, among other things, provide for and manage DOD's civil support mission. DOD generally does not acquire capabilities specifically for civil support, but it possesses a broad array of resources developed for its warfighting mission that could be brought to bear when civilian response capabilities are overwhelmed

---

[1] 42 U.S.C. § 5122 defines major disasters and emergencies. A major disaster is any natural catastrophe (including any hurricane, tornado, storm, high water, wind-driven water, tidal wave, tsunami, earthquake, volcanic eruption, landslide, mudslide, snowstorm, or drought), or regardless of cause, any fire, flood, or explosion, in any part of the United States, which in the determination of the President causes damage of sufficient severity and magnitude to warrant major disaster assistance to supplement the efforts and available resources of states, local governments, and disaster relief organizations in alleviating the damage, loss, hardship, or suffering caused thereby. An emergency is an occasion or instance for which, in the determination of the President, federal assistance is needed to supplement state and local efforts and capabilities to save lives and to protect property and public health and safety, or to lessen or avert the threat of a catastrophe in any part of the United States.

[2] For the purposes of this report, civil support refers to defense support of civil authorities, which is DOD's mission to provide support through the federal military force, National Guard, and other resources in response to requests for assistance from civil authorities for special events, domestic emergencies, designated law enforcement support, and other domestic activities.

GAO-13-763 Civil Support

or exhausted—or in instances where DOD offers unique capabilities. For example, DOD has been called upon to mitigate the effects of major disasters and emergencies by providing fuel and medical care, and certain military units within DOD may be tasked to provide specialized life-saving and decontamination capabilities in response to a radiological incident. The 2013 *Strategy for Homeland Defense and Civil Support*[3] recognizes that, although DOD is always in a support role to civilian authorities for disaster response, the capacity, capabilities, and training of the military mean that DOD often is expected to play a prominent supporting role in response efforts. The strategy also notes that public expectations for a rapid federal response have grown in the wake of major disasters such as Hurricane Katrina.

In July 2012,[4] the Secretary of Defense issued a memorandum directing the department to plan for a complex catastrophe—that is, an incident that results in cascading failures of critical infrastructure and causes extraordinary levels of casualties or damage. DOD has defined a complex catastrophe as a natural or man-made incident, including cyberspace attack, power grid failure, and terrorism, which results in cascading failures of multiple interdependent, critical, life-sustaining infrastructure sectors and causes extraordinary levels of mass casualties, damage, or disruption severely affecting the population, environment, economy, public health, national morale, response efforts, and/or government functions. A domestic incident of this scale is likely to affect multiple states even though DOD's definition of a complex catastrophe does not specifically include multiple states. An example of a complex catastrophe is the earthquake, tsunami, and nuclear reactor meltdown that struck Japan in 2011 and caused extensive loss of life and suffering. DOD said that the scope, scale and duration of Hurricane Sandy in 2012, which affected several states on the East Coast of the United States, fell short of the threshold for a complex catastrophe. According to Office of the Secretary of Defense officials, the department's increased focus on complex catastrophes is largely the result of lessons learned from a 2011 national-level planning exercise. This exercise tested the government's response to a large earthquake scenario that involved numerous

---

[3] Department of Defense, *Strategy for Homeland Defense and Civil Support* (Feb. 25, 2013).

[4] Secretary of Defense Memorandum, *Actions to Improve Defense Support in Complex Catastrophes* (July 20, 2012).

casualties, and caused widespread property damage and critical infrastructure degradation across eight states. A complex catastrophe has not yet occurred in the United States; however, if it does occur it would produce qualitative and quantitative effects that exceed those experienced in major disasters such as Hurricanes Katrina and Sandy, creating unprecedented demand for response capabilities at all levels of government.

In his July 2012 memorandum, the Secretary of Defense delineated nine major tasks (and 28 related sub-tasks) requiring departmental entities to: (1) define a complex catastrophe; (2) expedite access to reserve components; (3) better leverage immediate response authority;[5] (4) enable effective access to and use of all defense capabilities; (5) update DOD planning documents to include preparedness for complex catastrophes; (6) integrate and synchronize DOD planning with federal, regional, and state partners; (7) enable fastest identification of DOD capabilities for complex catastrophe response; (8) strengthen shared situational awareness, and (9) strengthen DOD preparedness through improvements to doctrine, exercises, training, and education. Most of the tasks and subtasks have a scheduled completion date, ranging from August 2012 to September 2014.

To date, we have published several reports on the progress DOD has made to address civil support issues. Among other things, these reports have focused on coordination between NORTHCOM and the states, the National Guard Bureau, and other federal agencies for civil support planning and response; capabilities requirements for civil support; National Guard requirements for responding to large-scale civil support incidents; DOD's planning, resourcing, and training for domestic chemical, biological, radiological, and nuclear incidents; NORTHCOM's civil support exercise program; and NORTHCOM's civil support guidance development and planning efforts. We recommended that DOD update its civil support strategy, doctrine, and DOD directives related to civil support and clarify roles and responsibilities for civil support personnel. The department generally concurred with these recommendations. These reports are listed in the Related GAO Products section at the end of this

---

[5] Immediate response authority allows DOD to provide immediate response to save lives, prevent human suffering, or mitigate great property damage under imminently serious conditions in response to a request from civil authorities when time does not permit approval from higher DOD headquarters.

GAO-13-763 Civil Support

report. You asked us to assess DOD's planning and capabilities for a complex catastrophe. This report examines the extent to which DOD has (1) planned for and identified capabilities to respond to complex catastrophes, and (2) established a command and control construct for complex catastrophes and other multistate incidents.

To determine the extent to which DOD has planned for and identified capabilities to respond to complex catastrophes, we assessed DOD civil support planning documents, guidance, and after action reports from civil support incidents and exercises that have occurred since 2011; and we met with Office of Secretary of Defense, Joint Staff, combatant command, military service, defense agency, and Reserve officials. We also met with several defense coordinating officers and Federal Emergency Management Agency (FEMA) officials to determine what planning was being conducted at the regional level. We also met with officials at NORTHCOM and U.S. Pacific Command (PACOM) to determine how the commands are incorporating a complex catastrophe scenario into civil support plans by the September 2013 and 2014 deadlines. We assessed planning guidance issued by the Joint Staff and Secretary of Defense and DOD joint doctrine against interviews with DOD and combatant command officials to determine how DOD was incorporating a complex catastrophe into civil support plans. To determine the extent to which DOD has established a command and control construct for complex catastrophes and other multistate incidents, we analyzed DOD doctrine and plans related to operational planning and command and control. We also reviewed laws and national-level policy pertaining to disaster response coordination and planning, and met with officials from the Office of the Secretary of Defense, the Joint Staff, NORTHCOM, PACOM, the military services, and the National Guard Bureau to determine DOD's existing command and control structure. In addition, we reviewed relevant documentation—including briefings, analyses, and after action reports related to Hurricane Sandy and National Level Exercise 2011—and met with Office of the Secretary of Defense, Joint Staff, combatant command, military service, and National Guard officials to determine the extent to which DOD had identified and analyzed multistate command and control issues. We also assessed DOD and interagency guidance and other documents including NORTHCOM's civil support plan, DOD's civil support joint publication and *Joint Action Plan for Developing Unity of Effort*, and DOD after action reports from Hurricane Sandy to determine how the existing command and control construct addressed complex catastrophes and other multistate incidents.

We conducted this performance audit from August 2012 to September 2013 in accordance with generally accepted government auditing standards. Those standards require that we plan and perform the audit to obtain sufficient, appropriate evidence to provide a reasonable basis for our findings and conclusions based on our audit objectives. We believe that the evidence obtained provides a reasonable basis for our findings and conclusions based on our audit objectives. More detailed information on our objectives, scope, and methodology can be found in appendix I of this report.

Background

Framework for Disaster Response

The federal government's response to major disasters and emergencies in the United States is guided by the Department of Homeland Security's *National Response Framework*.[6] The framework is based on a tiered, graduated response; that is, incidents are managed at the lowest jurisdictional level and supported by additional higher-tiered response capabilities as needed. Overall coordination of federal incident-management activities is generally the responsibility of the Department of Homeland Security. Within the Department of Homeland Security, FEMA is responsible for coordinating and integrating the preparedness of federal, state, local, and nongovernmental entities. In this capacity, FEMA engages in a range of planning efforts to prepare for and mitigate the effects of major disasters and emergencies. For example, FEMA is currently developing regional all-hazards and incident-specific plans intended to cover the full spectrum of hazards, including those that are more likely to occur in each region. FEMA expects to complete its current regional planning cycle by 2018.

Local and county governments respond to emergencies daily using their own capabilities and rely on mutual aid and other types of assistance agreements with neighboring governments when they need additional resources. For example, county and local authorities are likely to have the capabilities needed to adequately respond to a small-scale incident, such as a local factory explosion, and therefore would not request additional

---

[6] Department of Homeland Security, *National Response Framework* 2nd ed. (Washington, D.C.: May 2013).

resources. For larger-scale incidents, when resources are overwhelmed, local and county governments will request assistance from the state. States have resources, such as the National Guard of each state,[7]that they can marshal to help communities respond and recover. If additional capabilities are required, states may request assistance from one another through interstate mutual aid agreements, such as the Emergency Management Assistance Compact,[8] or the governors can seek federal assistance.

Various federal agencies play lead or supporting roles in responding to major disasters and emergencies, based on their authorities and capabilities, and the nature of the incident when federal assistance is required. For example, the Department of Energy is the lead federal agency for the reestablishment of damaged energy systems and components, and may provide technical expertise during an incident involving radiological and nuclear materials. DOD supports the lead federal agency in responding to major disasters and emergencies when (1) state, local, and other federal capabilities are overwhelmed, or unique defense capabilities are required; (2) it is directed to do so by the President or the Secretary of Defense; or (3) assistance is requested by the lead federal agency. When deciding whether to commit defense resources to a request for assistance by the lead federal agency, DOD evaluates the request against six criteria: legality, lethality, risk, cost, readiness, and appropriateness of the circumstances.[9]

---

[7] The Army and Air National Guard of the United States perform federal missions under the command of the President and the National Guard of each state performs state missions under the command of the state's governor. The National Guard can use available capabilities provided by DOD—such as transportation, engineering, medical, and communications—to respond to domestic emergencies while operating under the command of the governors.

[8] The Emergency Management Assistance Compact is a mutual aid agreement among member states and is administered by the National Emergency Management Association. States affected by major disasters and emergencies have increasingly relied on the Emergency Management Assistance Compact as a means to access resources from other states, including emergency managers, National Guard assets, and first responders.

[9] Joint Chiefs of Staff, Joint Pub. 3-28, *Defense Support of Civil Authorities* (Jul. 31, 2013).

DOD Organizations and Offices Involved in Major Disaster and Emergency Response

A number of DOD organizations have roles in planning for and responding to major disasters and emergencies.

- **The Assistant Secretary of Defense for Homeland Defense and Americas' Security Affairs**: The Assistant Secretary of Defense for Homeland Defense and Americas' Security Affairs serves as the principal civilian advisor to the Secretary of Defense on civil support issues.

- **The Joint Staff**: The Joint Staff coordinates with NORTHCOM and PACOM to ensure that civil support planning efforts are compatible with the department's war planning and advises the military services on the department's policy, training, and joint exercise development.

- **Combatant commands**: NORTHCOM and PACOM are responsible for carrying out the department's civil support mission, and have command and control authority depending on the location. The NORTHCOM area of responsibility for civil support is comprised of the contiguous 48 states, Alaska, and the District of Columbia. Outside of this area, NORTHCOM may also support civil authorities' major disaster and emergency response operations in the Commonwealth of Puerto Rico and the U.S. Virgin Islands. PACOM has these responsibilities for the Hawaiian Islands and U.S. territories in the Pacific.

- **Other Defense Organizations**: Other DOD organizations, such as the Army Corps of Engineers, the National Geospatial Intelligence Agency, and the Defense Logistics Agency, support FEMA during major disasters and emergencies by providing power generation capabilities, fuel, and logistics support as lead of several emergency support functions cited in the National Response Framework. The Army Corps of Engineers in particular serves as the lead for Emergency Support Function 3, Public Works and Engineering.

- **National Guard Bureau**: The National Guard Bureau serves as the channel of communications on all matters relating to the National Guard between DOD and the States.

In the aftermath of Hurricane Katrina, NORTHCOM assigned a defense coordinating officer with associated support staff (known as a defense coordinating element) in each of FEMA's 10 regional offices.[10] Defense coordinating officers are senior-level military officers with joint service experience, and training on the *National Response Framework* and the Department of Homeland Security's *National Incident Management System*.[11] Defense coordinating officers work closely with federal, state, and local officials to determine DOD's understanding of what additional or unique capabilities DOD can provide to mitigate the effects of a major disaster or emergency. Figure 1 shows the 10 FEMA regions.

---

[10] NORTHCOM has designated 10 defense coordinating officers, one in each of the 10 FEMA regions. Because FEMA Region IX is located in both NORTHCOM's and PACOM's areas of responsibility, PACOM has established two defense coordinating officers of its own, one for Hawaii and American Samoa, and one for Guam and the Northern Marianas.

[11] The *National Incident Management System* provides a systematic, proactive approach to guide departments and agencies at all levels of government, nongovernmental organizations, and the private sector to work seamlessly to prevent, protect against, respond to, recover from, and mitigate the effects of incidents, regardless of cause, size, location, or complexity, in order to reduce the loss of life and property and harm to the environment. The *National Incident Management System* works hand in hand with the *National Response Framework*.

Figure 1: Map of the Federal Emergency Management Agency Regions

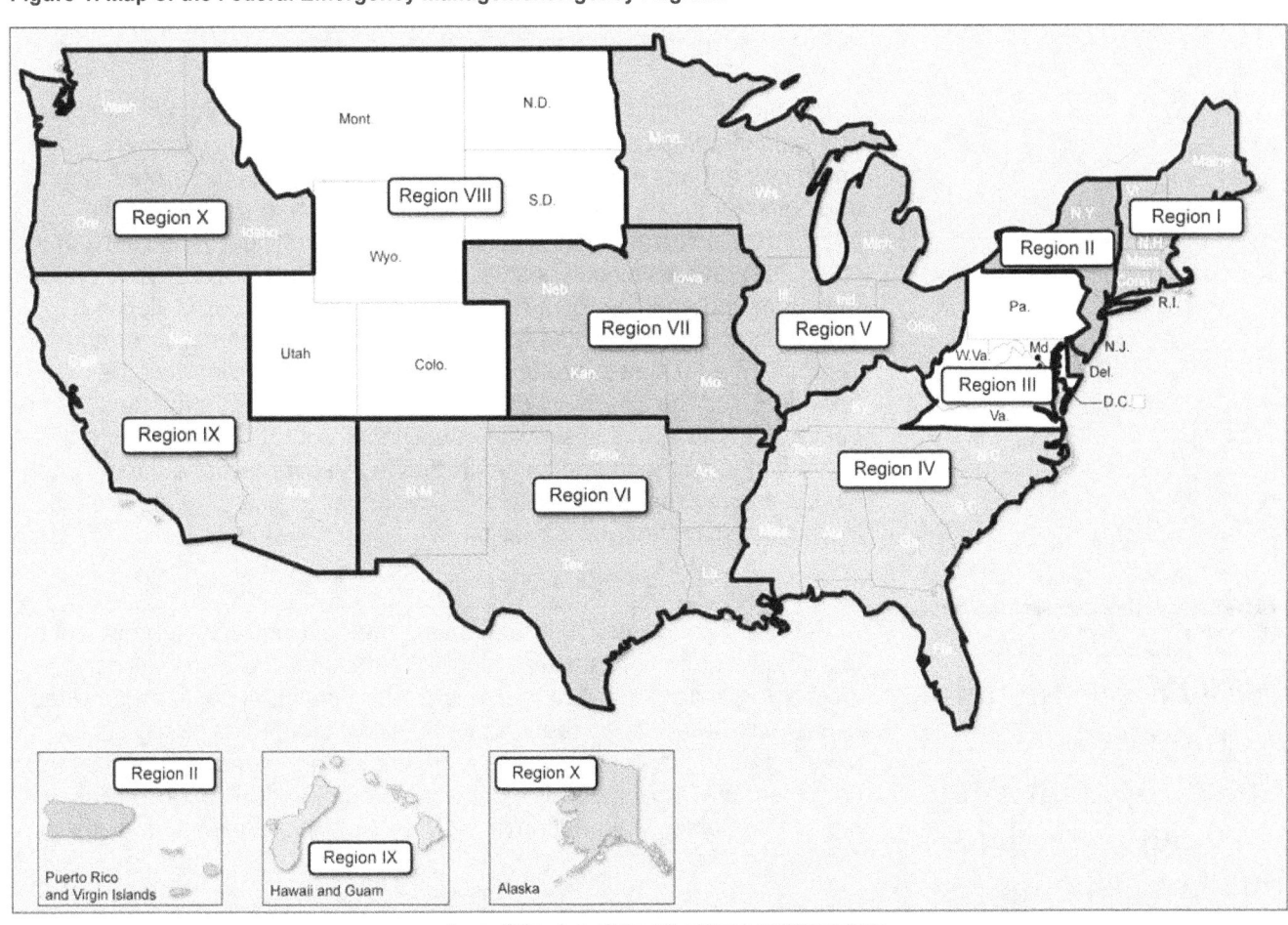

Source: GAO analysis of National Guard Bureau and DOD information.

The Dual-Status Commander Construct

According to DOD officials, dual-status commanders—active duty military or National Guard officers who coordinate state and federal responses to civil support incidents and events—have been used for select planned and special events since 2004, and more recently for civil support incidents. The dual-status commander construct provides the intermediate link between the federal and the state chains of command and is intended to promote unity of effort between federal and state forces to facilitate a rapid response to save lives, prevent human suffering, and protect property during major disasters and emergencies. The Secretary of Defense must authorize, and the Governor must consent to, designation of an officer to serve as a dual-status commander. During Hurricane Sandy, dual-status commanders served in New York, New Jersey, Maryland, Massachusetts, New Hampshire, and Rhode Island.

The National Defense Authorization Act for Fiscal Year 2012[12] provided that a dual-status commander should be the usual and customary command and control arrangement in situations when the armed forces and National Guard are employed simultaneously in support of civil authorities, including major disasters and emergencies. When serving in a title 32 or state active duty status, the National Guard of a state is under the command and control of the state's governor. DOD and National Guard personnel serving on federal active duty, sometimes referred to as being in Title 10 status, are under the command and control of the President and the Secretary of Defense. Dual-status commanders operate in both statuses simultaneously and report to both chains of command. Command and control refers to the exercise of authority and direction by a properly designated commander over assigned forces in the accomplishment of the mission.

NORTHCOM and PACOM Are Including a Complex Catastrophe in Their Civil Support Plans but Are Delaying Identification of Capability Requirements

NORTHCOM and PACOM are updating their existing civil support plans to include a complex catastrophe, as directed, but the plans will not identify capabilities needed to execute their plans that could be provided to execute the plans, as required, until FEMA completes its regional planning efforts in 2018. In the interim, combatant command officials have not determined how they will incorporate into their civil support plans regional capability information from those FEMA regions that have completed their plans.

---

[12] Pub. L. No. 112-81, § 515 (2011).

NORTHCOM and PACOM Are Updating Civil Support Plans to Address a Complex Catastrophe; But Are Not Identifying Capability Requirements Until FEMA's Regional Planning is Complete

NORTHCOM and PACOM are updating their civil support plans to include a complex catastrophe. However, the commands are delaying the identification of capabilities needed to execute the plans, as required by the Joint Staff, until FEMA completes its regional planning efforts. The Secretary of Defense's July 2012 memorandum directed NORTHCOM and PACOM to update their civil support plans—to include preparing for a complex catastrophe—by September 2013 and September 2014, respectively. In September 2012, the Joint Staff issued more specific guidance to the commands; directing them to, among other things, identify within the civil support plans required DOD forces and capabilities for responding to a complex catastrophe by the September 2013 and September 2014 deadlines.[13] NORTHCOM officials told us that they expect the command to update its civil support plan by September 2014, and that the plan would describe some general strategic-level complex catastrophe scenarios and identify general force requirements, such as the types of military units that would be needed to respond to a complex catastrophe. However, according to NORTHCOM officials, the command will not identify DOD capabilities that could be provided to civil authorities during a complex catastrophe until FEMA completes its plans.

According to PACOM officials, PACOM also expects to update its civil support plan by September 2014. These officials told us that PACOM's plan will describe a complex catastrophe scenario that begins with an infectious disease, followed by a typhoon that leads to an earthquake that triggers a tsunami. PACOM also plans to identify critical infrastructure likely to be impacted by this scenario. However, officials stated that PACOM's civil support plan will not identify capability needed to execute the plan, despite the requirement specified in the Joint Staff's planning guidance. Rather, NORTHCOM and PACOM plan to continue to work with FEMA to identify those DOD's capabilities that could be provided to respond to a complex catastrophe and include them in subsequent versions of the civil support plans once FEMA has completed its plans for each of the 10 FEMA regions during the next few years.

According to FEMA officials, DOD's civil support concept plans are intended to be coordinated with FEMA's regional all-hazards and incident-specific plans but these plans are not scheduled to be completed until

---

[13] Chairman of the Joint Chiefs of Staff, Defense Support to Civil Authorities Planning Order (September 25, 2012).

2018. FEMA is currently working with each of its regions to update both all-hazards and incident-specific plans, which are updated every 5 years. FEMA's all-hazards plans are intended to cover the spectrum of hazards, including accidents; natural disasters; terrorist attacks; and chemical, biological, nuclear, and radiological events. Incident-specific plans are intended to address those specific hazards that are believed to have a greater probability of occurring in a region when compared to other types of hazards and have unique response requirements. Each FEMA region has a collaborative team that is responsible for developing a regional all-hazards plan that details capabilities required at the regional level for supporting emergency response.

While FEMA's current efforts to develop regional plans are not scheduled to be completed until 2018, FEMA officials told us that their process to develop and update incident-specific plans is ongoing as needs arise in the regions. As of August 2013, half of the 10 FEMA regions had completed updating their all-hazards plan, and none of the 10 FEMA regions had completed updating their incident-specific plans. According to NORTHCOM officials, these FEMA regional plans are intended to, among other things, inform DOD of the local and state-level capabilities available for responding to a complex catastrophe in each FEMA region, as well as any capability gaps that might ultimately have to be filled by DOD or another federal agency.

DOD Officials Have Taken Some Initial Steps to Coordinate with FEMA to Develop Regional Capability Information; However, the Combatant Commands Have Not Determined How They Will Use This Information

DOD's defense coordinating officers have taken some initial steps to coordinate with FEMA; however, NORTHCOM, which is responsible for a majority of the civil support mission for DOD, has not determined how it will incorporate information produced by these efforts into its civil support plan. DOD has defense coordinating officers in each of FEMA's 10 regions who work closely with federal, state, and local officials to determine what specific capabilities DOD can provide to mitigate the effects of major disasters and emergencies when FEMA requests assistance. Defense coordinating officers are senior-level military officers with joint service experience, and training on the *National Response Framework* and the Department of Homeland Security's *National Incident Management System*. Currently they are coordinating with FEMA and other federal, state, and local agencies to determine regional and state capability requirements for a complex catastrophe in each of the regions. For example, the defense coordinating officer in FEMA Region IX, one of the regions that has completed its all-hazards plan, has helped the region develop bundled mission assignments for its regional plan that pre-identify a group of capabilities the region will require from DOD for a complex catastrophe to fill an identified capability gap, such as aircraft, communications, medical, and mortuary for responding to an earthquake in southern California. The bundled mission assignments are specific to the region's plans and are intended to expedite the process of preparing a request for assistance so that DOD can deliver the required capabilities more quickly. Similarly, within FEMA Region IV, which has also completed its all-hazards plan, the defense coordinating officer has helped to develop a list of specific response capabilities that DOD can plan to provide to civil authorities when needed. FEMA and the defense coordinating officers are exploring the possibility of developing bundled mission assignments for complex catastrophes for all of the FEMA regions. However, NORTHCOM and PACOM have not determined how this regional capability information will be incorporated into their civil support plans.

According to DOD doctrine, an effective whole of government approach is only possible when every agency understands the competencies and capabilities of its partners and works together to achieve common goals. This doctrine further states that DOD should interact with non-DOD agencies to gain a mutual understanding of their response capabilities and limitations.[14] By working through the defense coordinating officers to identify an interim set of specific capabilities that DOD could provide in response to a complex catastrophe—instead of waiting for FEMA to complete its five-year regional planning processes and then updating civil support plans—NORTHCOM and PACOM can enhance their preparedness and more effectively mitigate the risk of an unexpected capability gap during the five-year period until FEMA completes its regional plans in 2018.

---

[14] Joint Chiefs of Staff, Joint Pub. 3-08, *Interorganizational Coordination During Joint Operations.* (June 24, 2011).

A Gap Exists in DOD's Command and Control Framework for Complex Catastrophes and Other Multistate Incidents

DOD has established an overall command and control framework for a federal military civil support response. However, the command and control structure for federal military forces during incidents affecting multiple states such as complex catastrophes is unclear because DOD has not yet prescribed the roles, responsibilities, and relationships of command elements that may be involved in responding to such incidents.

DOD Has Established a Command and Control Framework for Responding to Federal Military Civil Support Incidents

DOD guidance and NORTHCOM civil support plans establish a framework for the command and control of federal military civil support, identifying a range of command elements and structures that may be employed depending on the type, location, magnitude, and severity of an incident, and the scope and complexity of DOD assistance. This framework addresses command and control for federal military forces operating independently or in parallel with state National Guard forces, and it also provides a model for the integrated command and control of federal military and state National Guard civil support.

DOD Has Established a Command and Control Structure for a Federal Military Civil Support Response

Joint Doctrine[15] and NORTHCOM's civil support concept plans collectively prescribe specific federal military command and control procedures and relationships for certain types of civil support incidents—such as radiological emergencies—and also identify potential command and control arrangements for incidents of varying scale. For example, for small-scale civil support responses, NORTHCOM's 2008 civil support concept plan[16] provides that a defense coordinating officer may be used to command and control federal military forces so long as the response force does not exceed the officer's command and control capability. Should an event exceed that threshold, a task force may be needed to command and control medium-scale military activities. Such a task force could be composed of personnel from a single military service; or, if the

---

[15] Joint Doctrine includes Joint Chiefs of Staff, Joint Pub. 3-28, *Defense Support of Civil Authorities*, (July 31, 2013); Joint Pub. 3-31, *Command and Control for Joint Land Operations*, (June 29, 2010); and Joint Pub. 3-33, *Joint Task Force Headquarters*, (July 30, 2012).

[16] U.S. Northern Command, Concept Plan 3501-08, *Defense Support of Civil Authorities* (Aug. 2008).

scope, complexity, or other factors of an incident require capabilities of at least two military departments, a joint task force may be established. The size, composition, and capabilities of a joint task force can vary considerably depending on the mission and factors related to the operational environment, including geography of the area, nature of the crisis, and the time available to accomplish the mission. For large-scale civil support responses, per the civil support concept plan, NORTHCOM can establish or expand an existing joint task force with multiple subordinate joint task forces, or appoint one or more of its land, air, or maritime functional component commanders to oversee federal forces. U.S. Army North, located at Fort Sam Houston, Texas, is NORTHCOM's joint force land component commander. Air Force North, located at Tyndall Air Force Base near Panama City, Florida, is NORTHCOM's joint force air component commander. U.S. Fleet Forces Command, located in Norfolk, Virginia, is NORTHCOM's joint force maritime component commander.

According to NORTHCOM's civil support concept plan, command and control of federal military forces providing civil support is generally accomplished using the functional component command structure. Within this structure, NORTHCOM transfers operational control[17] of federal military forces to a designated functional component commander. This commander may then deploy a subordinate task force or multiple task forces to execute command and control. For example, for land-based incidents, NORTHCOM would transfer operational control of federal forces to U.S. Army North, which could then deploy one or more of its subordinate command and control task forces. Figure 2 depicts a functional component command and control structure for a land-based federal military response to a major disaster or emergency in the NORTHCOM area of responsibility.

---

[17] Operational control is command authority over subordinate forces involving organizing and employing forces, assigning tasks, designating objectives, and giving direction necessary to accomplish a mission.

Figure 2: Functional Component Command and Control Structure for Land-based Federal Military Operations in the NORTHCOM Area of Responsibility

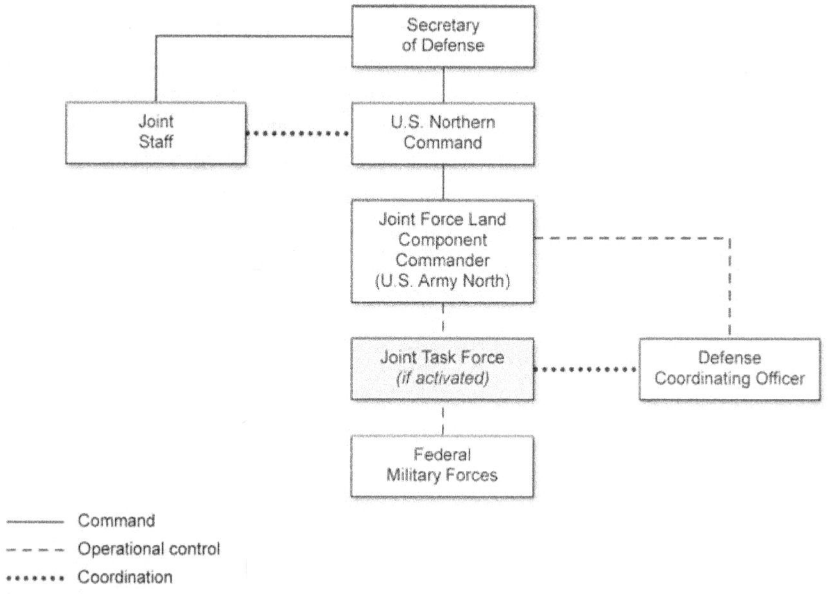

Command
Operational control
Coordination

Source: GAO analysis of DOD information.

DOD Has Established a Structure for Integrated Federal and State Military Command and Control

In certain cases, such as large-scale civil support responses, federal military and state National Guard forces may operate simultaneously in support of civil authorities. In such instances, a dual-status commander—with authority over both federal military forces and state National Guard forces—should be the usual and customary command arrangement. Federal military forces allocated to the dual-status commander through the request for assistance process are to be under that commander's control. For events or incidents that affect multiple states, a dual-status commander may be established in individual states. Dual status commanders do not have command and control over state National Guard forces in states that have not designated that commander as a dual status commander.

According to NORTHCOM's civil support concept plan, dual-status commanders provide the advantage of a single commander who is authorized to make decisions regarding issues that affect both federal and state forces under their command, thereby enhancing unity of effort. For example, dual-status authority allows the commander to coordinate and de-conflict federal and state military efforts while maintaining separate and distinct chains of command. Unlike some federal military task forces, dual-status commanders, when employed, are under the direct operational control of NORTHCOM, operating outside of the functional component command structure. Dual-status commanders also fall under a state chain-of-command that extends up through the state Adjutant General and Governor. Figure 3 depicts a command and control structure for a land-based, single-state federal military response to a major disaster or emergency in the NORTHCOM area of responsibility when a dual status commander is employed.

Figure 3: Dual-status Command and Control Structure for Single-State Land-based Operations in the NORTHCOM Area of Responsibility

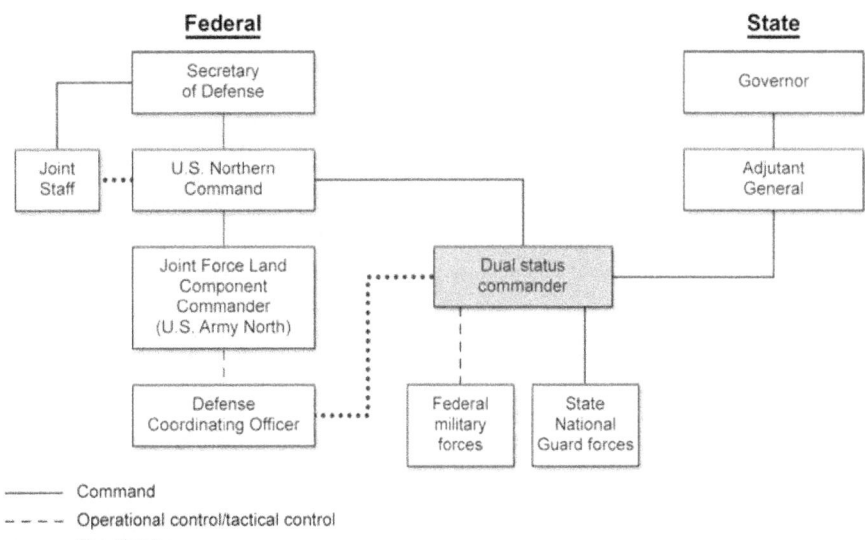

———— Command

– – – – Operational control/tactical control

•••••• Coordination

Source: GAO analysis of DOD information.

GAO-13-763 Civil Support

DOD Has Not Developed a Construct for the Command and Control of Federal Military Forces During Complex Catastrophes and Other Multistate Civil Support Incidents

The *Joint Action Plan for Developing Unity of Effort*[18] emphasizes the importance of properly configured command and control arrangements, and DOD doctrine[19] states that operational plans should identify the command structure expected to exist during their implementation. The Joint Action Plan also states that there is a likelihood that the United States will face a catastrophic incident affecting multiple states, and that past multistate emergencies demonstrated a coordinated and expeditious state-federal response is crucial in order to save and sustain lives. However, the command and control structure for federal military forces during multistate incidents is unclear because DOD has not yet prescribed the roles, responsibilities, and relationships among some of the command elements that may be involved in responding to such incidents. This gap in the civil support framework was illustrated by recent events such as National Level Exercise 2011—which examined DOD's response to a complex catastrophe in the New Madrid Seismic Zone— and the federal military response to Hurricane Sandy led by NORTHCOM in 2012. Citing this gap, officials we spoke with from across the department—including NORTHCOM, U.S. Army North, the Office of the Assistant Secretary of Defense for Homeland Defense and Americas' Security Affairs, the Joint Staff, and two of the defense coordinating elements—told us that the lack of a multistate command and control structure has created uncertainty regarding the roles and responsibilities of command elements that could be involved in response efforts.

National Level Exercise 2011

National Level Exercise 2011 simulated a major earthquake in the central United States region of the New Madrid Seismic Zone that caused widespread casualties and damage to critical infrastructure across eight states. The exercise took place in May 2011 and focused on integrated multi-jurisdictional catastrophic response and recovery activities between over 10,000 federal, regional, state, local, and private sector participants at more than 135 sites across the country.

Source: FEMA.

National Level Exercise 2011 helped to identify a gap in DOD's federal military command and control structure for multistate incidents. The exercise highlighted uncertainty regarding the roles and relationships among federal military command elements—and between such command elements and responding forces. For example, officials from U.S. Army North told us that the exercise revealed that not having a level of command between the dual-status commanders and NORTHCOM did not work well for such a large-scale, multistate incident, in part, because NORTHCOM, in the absence of an operational-level command element, faced challenges in managing the operations of federal military forces across a widespread area. According to DOD doctrine, operational-level commands, such as a functional component commander like the joint

---

[18] Department of Defense, Council of Governors, Department of Homeland Security, *Joint Action Plan for Developing Unity of Effort* (Washington, D.C.: 2011).

[19] Joint Chiefs of Staff, Joint Pub. 5-0, *Joint Operation Planning* (Aug. 2011).

force land component commander, can directly link operations to strategic objectives. To address this gap, two task forces were employed to operate between the dual-status commanders and NORTHCOM. While the task forces improved the overall command structure, according to Army officials, there was confusion regarding the role of the task forces in relation to the dual-status commanders, as well as federal military forces in states without a dual-status commander—which some of the state governors involved in this exercise chose not to appoint.

National Level Exercise 2011 illustrated other potential challenges associated with the lack of a multistate command and control structure. For example, according to NORTHCOM's publication on dual status commander standard operating procedures, NORTHCOM is responsible for coordinating the allocation of federal military forces among multiple states or areas—that is, determining where and how to employ federal military forces, particularly when there are similar requests for assistance. NORTHCOM officials told us that the command, looking at the totality of requests for assistance, would normally make such force employment determinations based on FEMA's prioritization of requests. However, in the absence of a multistate command and control structure to provide the necessary situational awareness over forces already engaged or available, NORTHCOM may be impaired in its ability to make additional informed decisions regarding the appropriate allocation of federal military resources. For example, at the outset of a complex catastrophe, DOD should expect to receive hundreds of requests with possibly redundant requirements and no prioritization. Similarly, a preliminary NORTHCOM analysis found that the current request for assistance process is unlikely to handle the timely demands that a complex catastrophe would incur, and that the prioritization of these requests would be unclear in the initial hours and days of the incident. Army officials told us that without an intermediate command entity to collate operational data and inform force allocation decisions, it was unclear how DOD would prioritize requests for federal military resources when there are multiple requests for the same or similar capabilities. Officials from the Joint Staff, and defense coordinating elements echoed these concerns, noting that it is unclear how DOD would prioritize the allocation of federal military forces across an affected multistate area when two or more dual-status commanders are in place.

Challenges associated with the lack of a multistate command and control construct were evident in the federal military response to Hurricane Sandy, which marked the first occasion in which multiple dual-status commanders were employed. For example, NORTHCOM officials told us that the command recognized the need for a command and control element between the dual-status commanders and NORTHCOM and, in early November 2012, employed a joint coordinating element—a concept without definition or doctrinal basis. According to DOD after action reports for Hurricane Sandy, the purpose of the joint coordinating element, employed as an extension of the joint force land component commander, was to aid in the coordination, integration, and synchronization of federal military forces. However, officials we spoke with from across the department told us that the joint coordinating element's role was neither well-defined nor well-communicated, rendering it largely ineffective. For example, officials from the Office of the Assistant Secretary of Defense for Homeland Defense and Americas' Security Affairs told us that uncertainty regarding the role of the joint coordinating element contributed to confusion during DOD's response to Hurricane Sandy.

Additionally, officials from one of the defense coordinating elements involved in the federal military response to Hurricane Sandy told us that the roles and responsibilities of the dual-status commander, joint coordinating element, and defense coordinating officer were unclear. According to these officials, such uncertainty hampered unity of command across state boundaries and created confusion regarding command and control relationships and force allocation across the affected multistate area. Officials from U.S. Army North and the Joint Staff similarly told us that there were challenges in allocating federal military forces during the response to Hurricane Sandy, in part, because of the command and control structure that was employed. Joint Staff officials noted that DOD's joint coordinating element had limited visibility and control over federal military forces.

DOD after action reports covering the federal military response to Hurricane Sandy also found that the command and control structure for federal military forces operating in the affected area was not clearly defined, resulting in the degradation of situational awareness and unity of effort, and the execution of missions without proper approval. For example, a U.S. Army North after action review concluded that while the joint coordinating element initially had a positive effect on situational awareness, inconsistencies in its purpose and task caused numerous problems. Table 1 shows select Hurricane Sandy after action report observations pertaining to command and control.

Table 1: Select Command and Control Observations Related to the Federal Military Response to Hurricane Sandy

After Action Report	Observation
NORTHCOM 2012 Hurricane Season After Action Report /Improvement Plan	- The command and control structure for dual-status commanders, the joint coordinating element, and higher headquarters was unclear to federal military personnel. - Command relationships were not initially clear to all personnel, and some missions were executed without the approval/awareness of the dual-status commander. - Authority of command with regard to the movement of forces was confusing. - The task and purpose of the joint coordinating element was not clearly identified. - There was not a well-defined chain of command or process to manage coordination of efforts of forces not assigned to a task force or dual-status commander.
U.S. Army North Hurricane Sandy After Action Report	- There was no defined structure between the defense coordinating element/officer, dual-status commander, and joint coordinating element; no one understood the role of the dual-status commander; and there was conflicting information received from the joint force land component command and the joint coordinating element. - The command and control structure needs to be clearly identified prior to forces arriving in the operating area. - Multiple defense coordinating officers were deployed to FEMA Region II, but no command relationships were established. This resulted in the degradation of DOD's situational awareness and unity of effort with FEMA.

Source: GAO analysis of DOD information.

According to NORTHCOM officials, the command has recognized the need for a multistate command and control construct, is analyzing this issue, and plans to incorporate the results of its analysis into the command's updated civil support concept plan by October 2013. NORTHCOM previously produced an analysis in March 2012 that identified a command and control gap for multistate incidents along with potential mitigation options, but this analysis was never approved. Also, we recommended in 2012 that DOD develop implementation guidance for the dual-status commanders that may partially address these challenges by covering, among other things, criteria for determining when and how to use dual-status commanders during civil support incidents affecting multiple states.[20] DOD agreed with this recommendation, and officials from the Office of the Assistant Secretary of Defense for Homeland Defense and Americas' Security Affairs told us that they are in the process of drafting such guidance. DOD has established a command and control framework for single-state civil support responses; but, until it

---

[20] GAO, *Homeland Defense: DOD Needs to Address Gaps in Homeland Defense and Civil Support Guidance*. GAO-13-128 (Washington, D.C.: Oct. 24, 2012).

develops, clearly defines, communicates, and implements a multistate command and control construct, federal military forces responding to a multistate event will likely face a range of operational ambiguities that could heighten the prospects for poorly synchronized response to major disasters and emergencies. For example, uncertainty regarding command structure may negatively affect the flow of information and prevent commanders from having adequate situational awareness over DOD's response, leading to reduced operational effectiveness and ineffective use of DOD forces. By identifying roles, responsibilities, and command relationships during multistate incidents such as complex catastrophes, DOD will be better positioned to manage and allocate forces across a multistate area, and ensure effective and organized response operations.

Conclusions

DOD acknowledged in its 2013 strategy for homeland defense and civil support that the department is expected to respond rapidly and effectively to civil support incidents, including complex catastrophes—incidents that would cause extraordinary levels of mass casualties and severely affect life-sustaining infrastructure. The effects of such an incident would exceed those caused by any previous domestic incident. NORTHCOM and PACOM, the combatant commands responsible for carrying out the department's civil support mission, cannot effectively plan for complex catastrophes in the absence of clearly defined capability requirements and any associated capability gaps. Consequently, DOD's decision to delay identifying capabilities that could be requested by civil authorities during a complex catastrophe until FEMA completes its five-year regional planning efforts may lead to a delayed response from DOD and ineffective intergovernmental coordination should a catastrophic event occur before 2018. An interim set of specific capabilities that DOD could refine as FEMA completes its regional planning process should help to mitigate the risk of a potential capability gap during a complex catastrophe. Further, developing, clearly defining, communicating, and implementing a command and control construct for federal military response to multistate civil support incidents would also likely enhance the effectiveness of DOD's response. National Level Exercise 11 and Hurricane Sandy highlighted this critical gap in command and control. Without a multistate command and control construct, DOD's response to a multistate incident, such as a complex catastrophe, may be delayed, uncoordinated, and could result in diminished efficacy.

Recommendations for Executive Action

We recommend that the Secretary of Defense take the following two actions:

(1) To reduce the department's risk in planning for a complex catastrophe and enhance the department's ability to respond to a complex catastrophe through at least 2018, direct the Commanders of NORTHCOM and PACOM to work through the defense coordinating officers to identify an interim set of specific DOD capabilities that could be provided to prepare for and respond to complex catastrophes while FEMA completes its five-year regional planning cycle.

(2) To facilitate effective and organized civil support response operations, direct the Commander of NORTHCOM—in consultation with the Joint Staff and Under Secretary of Defense for Policy, acting through the Assistant Secretary of Defense for Homeland Defense and Americas' Security Affairs—to develop, clearly define, communicate, and implement a construct for the command and control of federal military forces during multistate civil support incidents such as complex catastrophes—to include the roles, responsibilities, and command relationships among potential command elements.

Agency Comments and Our Evaluation

We provided a draft of this report to DOD for review and comment. DOD concurred with both recommendations and cited ongoing activities to address our recommendations. DOD's comments are reprinted in their entirety in appendix II. In addition, DOD provided technical comments, which we have incorporated into the report as appropriate.

DOD concurred with our recommendation to identify an interim set of specific capabilities that could be provided to prepare and respond to complex catastrophes. DOD stated that it recognizes the need for detailed planning to ensure the department can provide the needed capabilities, and is planning to work with defense coordinating officers and emergency support function leads to develop a set of capabilities. DOD also concurred with our recommendation to develop, clearly define, communicate, and implement a construct for command and control of federal military forces during multistate civil support incidents such as complex catastrophes. DOD stated that it recognizes the need for this and will ensure, as part of its contingency planning, that a range of command and control options are available for NORTHCOM and PACOM during multistate incidents. We believe that these actions will better position DOD to effectively and efficiently provide support during a complex catastrophe.

We also provided a draft of this report to DHS for review and comment. DHS provided technical comments, which were incorporated as appropriate.

As agreed with your offices, unless you publicly announce the contents of this report earlier, we plan no further distribution of this report until 30 days from the report date. At that time, we will distribute this report to the Secretary of Defense, the Acting Secretary of Homeland Security and other relevant officials. We are also sending copies of this report to interested congressional committees. The report is also available on our Web site at http://www.gao.gov.

If you or your staff have any questions about this report, please contact me at (202) 512-4523 or at leporeb@gao.gov. Contact points for our Offices of Congressional Relations and Public Affairs may be found on the last page of this report. Key contributors to this report are listed in Appendix III.

Brian J. Lepore
Director
Defense Capabilities and Management

Appendix I: Objectives, Scope, and Methodology

To determine the extent to which the Department of Defense (DOD) has planned for and identified capabilities to respond to a complex catastrophe, we assessed current DOD civil support planning documents, guidance, and after action reports from civil support incidents and exercises since 2011, and met with Office of Secretary of Defense, Joint Staff, combatant command, military service, defense agency, and Reserve officials. We assessed planning guidance issued by the Joint Staff and Secretary of Defense and DOD joint doctrine against interviews with DOD and combatant command officials to determine how DOD was incorporating a complex catastrophe into civil support plans. We also met with several defense coordinating officers and Federal Emergency Management Agency (FEMA) officials to determine what planning was being conducted at the regional level. We met with defense coordinating officers from regions that were impacted by Hurricane Sandy, participated in National Level Exercise 11, and completed their regional plans to gain an understanding of issues across a number of FEMA regions. NORTHCOM's deadline for completion of a complex catastrophe plan is September 2013 and U.S. Pacific Command (PACOM's) deadline is September 2014, which coincides with the commands' planning cycles. To determine NORTHCOM's and PACOM's planning requirements, we reviewed the July 2012 Secretary of Defense memorandum on complex catastrophes that requires NORTHCOM and PACOM to incorporate complex catastrophe scenarios into the commands' civil support plans and the Joint Staff planning order related to complex catastrophes. We compared planning requirements directed by the July 2012 Secretary of Defense memorandum on complex catastrophes and other applicable guidance to the federal and regional-level planning efforts to identify capabilities for a complex catastrophe. We met with officials at NORTHCOM and PACOM to determine how the commands are incorporating a complex catastrophe scenario into civil support plans by the September 2013 and September 2014 deadlines. Further, we reviewed recent GAO reports describing long-standing problems in planning and identifying civil support capabilities and gaps.

To determine the extent to which DOD has established a command and control construct for complex catastrophes and other multistate incidents, we analyzed DOD doctrine and plans related to operational planning and command and control. Specifically, we assessed DOD and interagency guidance including NORTHCOM's civil support plan, DOD's civil support joint publication, and *Joint Action Plan for Developing Unity of Effort* and DOD after action reports from Hurricane Sandy to determine how the existing command and control construct addressed complex catastrophes and other multistate incidents. We also reviewed laws relevant to disaster

response and domestic employment of federal military forces, including
the Stafford Act and certain provisions of Title 10 of the United States
Code, as well as national-level policy pertaining to response coordination
and planning, including the *National Response Framework*[1] and *National
Incident Management System*. In addition, we reviewed relevant
documentation—including briefings, analyses, and after action reports
related to Hurricane Sandy—and met with Office of the Secretary of
Defense, Joint Staff, combatant command, military service, and National
Guard officials to determine the extent to which DOD had analyzed
multistate command and control issues.

In addressing both of our audit objectives, we met with officials from the
DOD and the Department of Homeland Security organizations identified
in table 2.

Table 2: DOD and Department of Homeland Security Organizations Contacted

Name of Department	Organization
Department of Defense	Office of the Assistant Secretary of Defense for Homeland Defense and Americas' Security Affairs
	Office of the Assistant Secretary of Defense for Reserve Affairs
	The Joint Chiefs of Staff, Joint Directorate Antiterrorism/ Homeland Defense (J-34) Joint Directorate for Joint Force Development (J-7) Joint Directorate for Strategic Plans and Policy (J-5)
	The National Guard Bureau
	U.S. Northern Command, Colorado Springs, Colorado
	U.S. Army North, San Antonio, Texas
	Defense coordinating officers and staff Region II, New York City, New York
	Defense coordinating officers and staff Region III, Philadelphia, Pennsylvania
	Defense coordinating officers and staff Region IV, Atlanta, Georgia
	Defense coordinating officers and staff Region IX, Oakland, California
	U.S. Pacific Command, Honolulu, Hawaii
	Defense Logistics Agency
	U.S. Army Corps of Engineers
	U.S. Army Reserve Command

---

[1] Department of Homeland Security, *National Response Framework* 2nd *ed* (Washington, D.C.: May 2013).

Name of Department	Organization
Department of Homeland Security	Federal Emergency Management Agency, National Preparedness Directorate
	Federal Emergency Management Agency, Response Directorate

Source: GAO.

Note: Unless otherwise indicated, these organizations are located within the Washington, D.C. metropolitan area.

We conducted this performance audit from August 2012 to September 2013 in accordance with generally accepted government auditing standards. Those standards require that we plan and perform the audit to obtain sufficient, appropriate evidence to provide a reasonable basis for our findings and conclusions based on our audit objectives. We believe that the evidence obtained provides a reasonable basis for our findings and conclusions based on our audit objectives.

Appendix II: Comments from the Department of Defense

OFFICE OF THE ASSISTANT SECRETARY OF DEFENSE
2600 DEFENSE PENTAGON
WASHINGTON, D.C. 20301-2600

HOMELAND DEFENSE
& AMERICAS' SECURITY AFFAIRS

SEP 2 3 2013

Mr. Brian J. Lepore
Director, Defense Capabilities and Management
U.S. Government Accountability Office
441 G Street, N.W.
Washington, DC 20548

Dear Mr. Lepore:

This is the Department of Defense (DoD) response to the GAO draft report, GAO 13-763, "CIVIL SUPPORT: Actions are Needed to Improve DoD's Planning for a Complex Catastrophe," dated September 2013 (GAO Code 351770). DoD concurs with both recommendations. Responses to the recommendations are enclosed.

Our point of contact for this action is Mr. Sam Binkley, Office of the Assistant Secretary of Defense for Homeland Defense and Americas' Security Affairs (OASD (HD&ASA)), (571) 256-8318 or samuel.g.binkley.civ@mail.mil.

Sincerely,

Todd M. Rosenblum
Principal Deputy Performing the Duties of the
Assistant Secretary of Defense

Enclosure:
As stated

GAO DRAFT REPORT DATED SEPTEMBER 2013
GAO-13-763 (GAO CODE 351770)

"CIVIL SUPPORT: Actions are Needed to Improve DoD's Planning for a
Complex Catastrophe"

DEPARTMENT OF DEFENSE COMMENTS
TO THE GAO RECOMMENDATIONS

RECOMMENDATION 1: The Secretary of Defense direct the Commanders of
NORTHCOM and PACOM to work through the defense coordinating officers to
identify an interim set of specific DoD capabilities that could be provided to
prepare for and respond to complex catastrophes while FEMA completes its five-
year regional planning cycle.

DoD RESPONSE: Concur.
DoD recognizes the need for detailed planning to ensure the Department can
provide the necessary capabilities in support of civil authorities during a complex
catastrophe. DoD actively plans for Defense Support of Civil Authorities (DSCA)
in response to major disasters, and these planning efforts continue to evolve as part
of the ongoing work to prepare the Department for complex catastrophes.

DoD has pre-identified response capabilities in the DSCA execute order
(EXORD); the chemical, biological, radiological, and nuclear EXORD;
USNORTHCOM and USPACOM DSCA contingency plans; and FEMA's pre-
scripted mission assignment catalog. While the capabilities identified in those
documents will not comprise the entirety of a DoD response during a complex
catastrophe, they will be available as initial capabilities as FEMA continues to
identify requirements. Additional available capabilities within the DoD inventory
may be provided upon request.

The Secretary of Defense recently directed the Chairman of the Joint Chiefs of
Staff to coordinate the development of an enduring planning framework resulting
in DoD all-hazards regional response operations plans. Defense Coordinating
Officers, in support of the Combatant Commands, will play an integral role in the
development of these regional plans and the identification of specific support
capabilities. DoD will also continue working with national-level Emergency
Support Function leadership to identify DoD capabilities that civil authorities
might request during a complex catastrophe.

2

RECOMMENDATION 2: The Secretary of Defense direct the Commander of
NORTHCOM—in consultation with the Joint Staff and Under Secretary of
Defense for Policy, acting through the Assistant Secretary of Defense for
Homeland Defense and Americas' Security Affairs—to develop, clearly define,
communicate, and implement a construct for the command and control of federal
military forces during multistate civil support incidents such as complex
catastrophes—to include the roles, responsibilities, and command relationships
among potential command elements.

DoD RESPONSE: Concur.
DoD agrees that a clearly defined, well communicated construct for the command
and control (C2) of Federal military forces will facilitate effective and organized
DoD support of the lead Federal Department or Agency and the Federal
Coordinating Officer. USNORTHCOM, in particular, has identified C2 as a major
focus area in its planning for complex catastrophes, and has provided both a
Commander's Estimate for C2 and conducted a C2 Table Top Exercise to better
define roles and responsibilities.

DoD will ensure, through its contingency planning process, that the range of C2
options identified in USNORTHCOM and USPACOM contingency plans are
sufficient for multistate incidents, to include complex catastrophes, in support of
the National Response Framework. Combatant Commands will continue to be
responsible for ensuring that the C2 architecture for each incident is appropriate
based on factors including, but not limited to, type of incident, requirements, and
available DoD forces and capabilities.

Appendix III: GAO Contact and Staff Acknowledgements

GAO Contact	Brian Lepore, Director, (202) 512-4523, leporeb@gao.gov
Staff Acknowledgments	In addition to the contact named above Marc Schwartz, Assistant Director; Tracy Burney; Ryan D'Amore; Susan Ditto; Gina Flacco; Michael Silver; Amie Steele; and Michael Willems made key contributions to this report.

Related GAO Products

Homeland Defense: DOD Needs to Address Gaps in Homeland Defense and Civil Support Guidance. GAO-13-128. Washington, D.C.: October 24, 2012.

Homeland Defense: Continued Actions Needed to Improve Management of Air Sovereignty Alert Operations. GAO-12-311. Washington, D.C.: January 31, 2012.

Homeland Defense and Weapons of Mass Destruction: Additional Steps Could Enhance the Effectiveness of the National Guard's Life Saving Response Forces. GAO-12-114. Washington, D.C.: December 7, 2011.

Homeland Defense: Actions Needed to Improve Planning and Coordination for Maritime Operations. GAO-11-661. Washington, D.C.: June 22, 2011.

Intelligence, Surveillance, and Reconnaissance: DOD Needs a Strategic, Risk-Based Approach to Enhance Its Maritime Domain Awareness. GAO-11-621. Washington, D.C.: June 20, 2011.

Homeland Defense: DOD Needs to Take Actions to Enhance Interagency Coordination for Its Homeland Defense and Civil Support Missions. GAO-10-364. Washington, D.C.: March 30, 2010.

Homeland Defense: DOD Can Enhance Efforts to Identify Capabilities to Support Civil Authorities during Disasters. GAO-10-386. Washington, D.C.: March 30, 2010.

Homeland Defense: Planning, Resourcing, and Training Issues Challenge DOD's Response to Domestic Chemical, Biological, Radiological, Nuclear and High-Yield Explosive Incidents. GAO 10-123. Washington, D.C.: October 7, 2009.

Homeland Defense: U.S. Northern Command Has a Strong Exercise Program, but Involvement of Interagency Partners and States Can Be Improved. GAO-09-849. Washington, D.C.: September 9, 2009.

National Preparedness: FEMA Has Made Progress, but Needs to Complete and Integrate Planning, Exercise, and Assessment Efforts. GAO-09-369. Washington, D.C.: April 30, 2009.

Emergency Management: Observations on DHS's Preparedness for Catastrophic Disasters. GAO-08-868T. Washington, D.C.: June 11, 2008.

National Response Framework: FEMA Needs Policies and Procedures to Better Integrate Non-Federal Stakeholders in the Revision Process. GAO-08-768. Washington, D.C.: June 11, 2008.

Homeland Defense: Steps Have Been Taken to Improve U.S. Northern Command's Coordination with States and the National Guards Bureau, but Gaps Remain. GAO-08-252. Washington, D.C.: April 16, 2008.

Homeland Defense: U.S. Northern Command Has Made Progress but Needs to Address Force Allocation, Readiness Tracking Gaps, and Other Issues. GAO-08-251. Washington, D.C.: April 16, 2008.

Continuity of Operations: Selected Agencies Tested Various Capabilities during 2006 Governmentwide Exercise. GAO-08-105. Washington, D.C.: November 19, 2007.

Homeland Security: Preliminary Information on Federal Action to Address Challenges Faced by State and Local Information Fusion Centers. GAO-07-1241T. Washington, D.C.: September 27, 2007.

Homeland Security: Observations on DHS and FEMA Efforts to Prepare for and Respond to Major and Catastrophic Disasters and Address Related Recommendations and Legislation. GAO-07-1142T. Washington, D.C.: July 31, 2007.

Influenza Pandemic: DOD Combatant Commands' Preparedness Efforts Could Benefit from More Clearly Defined Roles, Resources, and Risk Mitigation. GAO-07-696. Washington, D.C.: June 20, 2007.

Homeland Security: Preparing for and Responding to Disasters. GAO-07-395T. Washington, D.C.: March 9, 2007.

Catastrophic Disasters: Enhanced Leadership, Capabilities, and Accountability Controls Will Improve the Effectiveness of the Nation's Preparedness, Response, and Recovery System. GAO-06-903. Washington, D.C.: September 6, 2006.

Homeland Defense: National Guard Bureau Needs to Clarify Civil Support Teams' Mission and Address Management Challenges. GAO-06-498. Washington, D.C.: May 31, 2006.

Hurricane Katrina: Better Plans and Exercises Needed to Guide the Military's Response to Catastrophic Natural Disasters. GAO-06-643. Washington, D.C.: May 15, 2006.

Hurricane Katrina: GAO's Preliminary Observations Regarding Preparedness, Response, and Recovery. GAO-06-442T. Washington, D.C.: March 8, 2006.

Emergency Preparedness and Response: Some Issues and Challenges Associated with major Emergency Incidents. GAO-06-467T. Washington, D.C.: February 23, 2006.

GAO'S Preliminary Observations Regarding Preparedness and Response to Hurricanes Katrina and Rita. GAO-06-365R. Washington, D.C.: February 1, 2006.

Homeland Security: DHS' Efforts to Enhance First Responders' All-Hazards Capabilities Continue to Evolve. GAO-05-652. Washington, D.C.: July 11, 2005.

Homeland Security: Process for Reporting Lessons Learned from Seaport Exercises Needs Further Attention. GAO-05-170. Washington, D.C.: January 14, 2005.

GAO's Mission	The Government Accountability Office, the audit, evaluation, and investigative arm of Congress, exists to support Congress in meeting its constitutional responsibilities and to help improve the performance and accountability of the federal government for the American people. GAO examines the use of public funds; evaluates federal programs and policies; and provides analyses, recommendations, and other assistance to help Congress make informed oversight, policy, and funding decisions. GAO's commitment to good government is reflected in its core values of accountability, integrity, and reliability.
Obtaining Copies of GAO Reports and Testimony	The fastest and easiest way to obtain copies of GAO documents at no cost is through GAO's website (http://www.gao.gov). Each weekday afternoon, GAO posts on its website newly released reports, testimony, and correspondence. To have GAO e-mail you a list of newly posted products, go to http://www.gao.gov and select "E-mail Updates."
Order by Phone	The price of each GAO publication reflects GAO's actual cost of production and distribution and depends on the number of pages in the publication and whether the publication is printed in color or black and white. Pricing and ordering information is posted on GAO's website, http://www.gao.gov/ordering.htm. Place orders by calling (202) 512-6000, toll free (866) 801-7077, or TDD (202) 512-2537. Orders may be paid for using American Express, Discover Card, MasterCard, Visa, check, or money order. Call for additional information.
Connect with GAO	Connect with GAO on Facebook, Flickr, Twitter, and YouTube. Subscribe to our RSS Feeds or E-mail Updates. Listen to our Podcasts. Visit GAO on the web at www.gao.gov.
To Report Fraud, Waste, and Abuse in Federal Programs	Contact: Website: http://www.gao.gov/fraudnet/fraudnet.htm E-mail: fraudnet@gao.gov Automated answering system: (800) 424-5454 or (202) 512-7470
Congressional Relations	Katherine Siggerud, Managing Director, siggerudk@gao.gov, (202) 512-4400, U.S. Government Accountability Office, 441 G Street NW, Room 7125, Washington, DC 20548
Public Affairs	Chuck Young, Managing Director, youngc1@gao.gov, (202) 512-4800 U.S. Government Accountability Office, 441 G Street NW, Room 7149 Washington, DC 20548

Please Print on Recycled Paper.